Bernard of Hollywood™ PIN-UPS:

Brunettes!

SUSAN BERNARD

WARNER 🆆 TREASURES™

PUBLISHED BY WARNER BOOKS

A TIME WARNER COMPANY

*I have tried my very best to correctly identify
all my father's photographic subjects and apologize
if there is an error.*

Warner Books, Inc.,
1271 Avenue of the Americas
New York, NY 10020

 A Time Warner Company

Book design by Lisa C. McGarry

Printed in Mexico
First Printing: March 1995
10 9 8 7 6 5 4 3 2 1

ISBN: 0-446-91004-X

For my son, Joshua Miller

"I dream of Jeanie with the light brown hair,
Floating, like a vapor, on the soft summer air."
—STEPHEN COLLINS FOSTER

In my search for Brunettes, cross-checking photo files, and researching the ancestries of these lovelies, I realized my father had photographed some of his most infectious subjects over several decades, and I was fascinated to find how many, at one time or another, were Brunettes. I even found '30s photographs of my own mother in Paris, when she was starring in the Earl Carroll Vanities—her long red hair was painted shiny blue-black.

Sorting through the massive collection of Bernard of Hollywood's Brunettes, I found exteriors and interiors, intertwining knowns and unknowns, color and black and white, torrid temptresses and cuddly cuties. I tossed them about, gave them names: Slow Burn, Paris Calling!, Cola Coquette, Hot Toddy. Fluctuating costumes and backgrounds, composition and lighting. I hope I've recaptured the enormous impact these nostalgic, and often camp, lovelies promised.

Julie Newmar

"START THE SHOW"

Gene Tierney

"SUNKISSED"

Laurette Luez

"GOOD CONNECTION"

Mara Corday

"OH MY!"

Jane Greer

"ACROSS THE BOARD"

Maryann Baird

"PARIS CALLING!"

Ann Miller

"SAVE ME!"

Ann Melton

"COLA COQUETTE"

Mitzi Gaynor

"WHITE CHIFFON"

Jo Jordan

"SLOW BURN"

Gwenn Caldwell

"DESIGN FOR LOVING"

Marla English

"LIGHTS OUT"

Ann Melton

"CRAZY OVER YOU"

Osa Mason

"HOT TODDY"

Ann Miller

"YOUR MOVE"

Minka Diaz

"BRANCHING OUT"

Marla English

"ON MY KNEES"

Vivian Mason

"STARS AND STRIPES"

Minka Diaz

"DESERT STORM"

Marilyn Monroe

"SEASIDE STAR"

Laurette Luez

"TROPICALE"

Jo Jordan

"RECOMMENDED REEDING"

Ann Melton

"BLACK MAGIC"

Rosemarie Bowe

"GOT A LIGHT?"

Janet Leigh

"GIRL NEXT DOOR"

Mara Corday

"BEDTIME!"

Mara Corday

"BEAUTY AND THE BEACH"

Ann Melton

"LAST SIP"

Many have contributed to making these publications possible: I am especially grateful to Bob Tabian, my agent, and my editor, Karen Kelly.

I owe special thanks to my assistant, Leslie Larson, and also Rod Vulich, Sygma photo agency, John Reichman, Mark Olbrich, Russell Adams, Theron Kabrich, John Gieo, London's Christie's, Ken Norwick, and my longtime legal guardian angel, Arthur Stashower.

Foremost, I am truly appreciative to my mother and father.